MW00680229

IT TAKES A
FAMILY
TO RAISE A
YOUTH
MINISTRY

Developing an Effective Strategy for Serving Families

MIKE JUSTICE

Beacon Hill Press of Kansas City
Kansas City, Missouri

EXECUTIVE EDITOR
D'Wayne Leatherland

EDITORIAL ASSISTANTS
John Schinkel
Julia Farrell

COVER DESIGN
Kevin Williamson

Copyright 1998
Beacon Hill Press of Kansas City
ISBN 083-411-7347

All Scripture quotations, unless otherwise indicated, are taken
from the *Holy Bible, New International Version*® (NIV®). Copyright ©
1973, 1978, 1984 by International Bible Society. Used by permission of Zondervan Publishing House. All rights reserved.

This book is dedicated to

My mom and dad
for giving me a strong sense of family.

My wife, Lois,
for sharing life with me
and building a family with me.

My former Sunday School teachers and youth workers
for investing their lives in me.

The churches where I have served
for allowing me to minister to their families with teens.

God, my Heavenly Father,
whose grace has saved me, called me,
and formed me into who I am.

Contents

An Introduction to Ministry to Families with Teens

*L*et me tell you where I got my interest in ministering to families with teens. First, there was the day I was in my office, doing the usual stuff (planning the next retreat, getting ready for the next Wednesday night, wishing I was playing golf, etc.) when I got a phone call from Diane, the mom of one of my teens. She told me there had been some problems around their house—Steve, her son, wasn't following "the rules" anymore. She wanted to bring Steve; her husband, Bill (Steve's stepfather); and their daughter, Michelle, into my office for some counseling. I wasn't equipped for that. It was my first youth ministry position, and I hadn't gone to school for that kind of stuff. But they were planning to come in the next evening.

Then there were the Jacobs, a single mother with her two teenagers and two younger children. They lived a couple of doors down from our church. One of the teens attended youth group activities occasionally; the mom, Vicki, came to church a couple of times a year; and the other teen never came to church. Vicki came to me one day in desperation, looked directly at me, and asked what my church had to offer her and her family. She "needed help," she said, so she came to the one place she had always heard would "be there to help." Ryan, her oldest son, was about to go down "the wrong road," and she could see the future coming. Her first husband was in jail. She was afraid her son would soon join him. I had to do something to help her.

Finally, there were the Stephensons, a family that was very active in my church. The parents were some of my strongest supporters. They fit the traditional family mold; they came to church to be fed and to learn how to grow as individuals and as a family. They challenged me to provide opportunities that stretched them—both as individual Christians and as parents. The Stephensons were genuinely concerned about the spiritual health of their family and were committed to doing whatever it took to continue this growth together.

Can you relate? You probably know some Steves and Ryans. You've probably had to deal with the needs expressed by parents such as Diane and Vicki. And if you're blessed, you've got several families like the Stephensons in your church. Different names but the same needs.

You and I are called to help meet those needs. I learned to become family-friendly not by choice but out of necessity. I had no idea *what* I was doing or how it would change what I was doing.

Have you, too, realized that you need to begin considering the needs of families more in your youth ministry? If you're like me, you may not even know what that *really* means. Will the shift simply require a title change, or should you prepare for a significant overhaul of your current youth ministry program?

It Takes a Family to Raise a Youth Ministry is written for you. You're familiar with the frustrations. You've grown tired of skirting around issues and conflicts. You know that something needs to be done to bridge the gaps between you, your youth, and their families. But what? And how? Maybe you're just not certain your church is ready for such a shift. Maybe you're not even sure *you* are.

What you need is a plan, a strategy. *It Takes a Family to Raise a Youth Ministry* is just that: a guide to developing an effective strategy for serving families. Throughout this book, you'll discover the benefits and joys of ministering to your youth within the context of the most powerful influence in their lives: their families.

You'll be guided step-by-step through the process of developing your own family ministry philosophy, unique to the individual needs and circumstances of your own ministry setting. You'll examine existing family ministry models for ideas on what might work for you. And you'll find an easy-to-follow plan for implementing the first stages of your new ministry mind-set.

It Takes a Family to Raise a Youth Ministry will help you put into place the elements that will work perfectly for your church's youth ministry. We'll first discuss what constitutes an acceptable foundation for a ministry to families with teens; we'll also examine today's family and some of their needs. Part 1 will help you gain some footholds as you lay your foundation for this new ministry approach. There may come a time when someone will question why you made a change to this new ministry, and part 1 will help you answer those questions. Part 2 will explore how to make the transition from a traditional youth ministry approach to one that includes ministering to families within the context of youth ministry.

We've included Family Strategy Builders along the way to assist you in developing your own game plan for implementing your ministry to families with teens. Not everyone's church is the same. Circumstances, environments, and needs are different; therefore, the responses to these questions—and the implications for your ministry—will be different. These questions will enable you to design a ministry to families with teens that will adapt perfectly to your church's unique makeup.

As an added bonus, we've included some ready-to-use parent/teen talks from some well-known veteran youth workers; use these to conduct your own parent/teen meetings, retreats, or classes. The talks cover different topics that relate to family life and can be used in a variety of settings. You'll find these practical and easy to use as you begin to raise your youth ministry to another level.

So don't wait any longer. Keep reading to find out why it really does take a family to raise a youth ministry!

Part one

It Takes a Family

When it's time for newly hatched eaglets to learn to fly, the mother eagle puts the young eaglet on her back and flies to a great height. Once they reach the necessary height, the young eaglet opens its wings and soars off its mother's back. The eaglet begins to fly, with its mother directly below. Since flying is something new to the eaglet, it does not yet have the endurance required to fly long distances. So when the eaglet gets tired, it lands again on its mother's back. Over time and with practice, the eaglet gains strength and learns to fly. It learns to fly by watching an example, by following that example, and then, over time, by becoming like that example—able to fly on its own.

Research continues to show that, for better or worse, a teen's family represents the most influential network of earthly relationships in his or her life. For this simple reason, we believe that the most effective youth ministry always takes place in the context of the family.

—Tom Lytle, Kelly Schwartz, and Gary Hartke—
101 Ways to Be Family-Friendly in Youth Ministry

Why "Family Ministry"?

*I*t's a fact. Regardless of the number of hours a youth worker spends with teens, the quality of a church's youth programming, or the number of mountaintop experiences a youth leader shares with a teen, *nobody* has a greater impact on a teen's spiritual development than his or her parent(s). Mark DeVries, author of *Family-Based Youth Ministry,* says it this way: "Just as gravity pulls objects toward the ground, whether we want it to or not, so families have unparalleled influence on the development of their [teens'] lives and character."[1]

What better way for a church to minister to the needs of teens than by utilizing the most influential people in the teens' lives—their parents!

When we see teens as integral parts of a family system —not isolated from it—our ministry to them takes on different expressions and approaches. A good symbol for the family is a three-dimensional hanging mobile that hangs above a baby crib. When one of the hanging pieces is moved, all the pieces of the mobile begin to rock and twist. Now replace the pieces of the mobile with members of a family—a mom, a dad, a couple of teens. When one member of the family begins moving, the other family members are impacted as well, causing them to also begin moving. Even extended family members (grandparents, aunts, uncles, cousins) are often part of the perpetually moving mobile.

When you minister to one part of the family (the teen), other parts of the family are directly affected. Traditionally, though, the church has separated the members of a family and ministered to them in isolation. An isolationist approach to youth ministry, however, is simply ineffective.

Are you ready to examine *why* it takes a family to raise your youth ministry? Let's find out!

chapter one

Building a Foundation

$\mathcal{I}$n order to understand why you should make the move to ministering to families with teens, it's critical to make certain that what is meant by *family* is clearly understood. Let's begin by examining God's Word to review *(a)* where families came from, *(b)* the biblical blueprints for the various relationships within the family, and *(c)* how the Church provides examples of God's plan for family.

In the Beginning . . .

God instituted family in Genesis 1. He gave Eve to Adam and commanded them to be fruitful and multiply. Then came Cain and Abel—and the first family was born. It wasn't perfect. It wasn't without its challenges. But the family was the first institution God ordained. The only other institution ordained by God was the Church. It only makes sense that these two God-ordained institutions should work together to fulfill His purposes.

Throughout the Bible, however, there's no clear definition of the word *family*. Interestingly, the Hebrew language has no actual word for *family*. The New Testament Greek word *oîkos*, meaning "household," is often translated "family" and refers to everyone living in a house (including servants and various relatives). It seems to me that these folks felt that relationships were as important as bloodlines. Those who had grown close to them were considered family as much as those who were their biological family members. So, from this we can gather that the definition of family can extend far beyond just moms and dads, brothers and sisters, to include others who are closely involved with the family, such as friends and neighbors.

Blueprints

Although there is no God-ordained definition of family, the Bible does have something to say about family. Throughout Scripture, God calls us into a relationship with Him. He also wants our relationship with Him to influence the other relationships we're a part of—especially those among family members.

The Bible teaches that God's ideal environment for spiritual nurture is located in the home. In Deuteronomy 6:4-9 parents are instructed to teach their children about God in all aspects of daily life. Ephesians 6:4 places the responsibility for spiritual nurture in the home by stat-

> *No matter where you look in our Judeo-Christian heritage, it is the parents who have the prime responsibility to bring up their children in the faith.*
>
> John Westerhoff
> *Bringing Up Children in the Faith, 7*

ing, "Fathers, . . . bring [your children] up in the training and instruction of the Lord." It's necessary, therefore, that we, as ministers, equip parents to disciple their teens.

Within the family, various relationships are continually competing for time and attention. It's important that we have a solid knowledge of these lines of connectedness in order to effectively communicate with and minister to the individual family members.

God reveals, in Genesis 2:24, the priority of the relationship between a husband and wife by establishing the divine origin of marriage. In Matthew 19:4-6, Jesus refers to this foundational statement when noting the permanence of marriage as a part of God's order in creation. Although divorce was not part of God's initial plan, divorce does occur, and everyone involved feels the effects. In order for the church to be an arm of God's redemptive grace, it needs to address the effects of divorce and minister to those affected—while still upholding marriage as God's original and ideal design.

In Exodus 20:12, God commands the honoring of fathers and

mothers. This is not just a commandment for young children. We are to show honor to our parents through our treatment and care for them as long as they live. In Mark 7:9-13, Jesus emphasized the importance of family relationships when He told the Pharisees they had nullified the Word of God by not taking care of their parents (even though their parents were adults themselves). In 1 Timothy 5:3-4, Paul tells Timothy to make sure widows are cared for properly. Their children and grandchildren should "put their religion into practice by caring for their own family and so repaying their parents and grandparents, for this is pleasing to God." A ministry to families with teens needs to be sensitive to ministering intergenerationally. For example, by including senior adults as sponsors for activities or as part of the teens' ministry, both the teens and the senior adults benefit from the relationships formed through this interaction.

The Family of God

The relationship between the Church and the family should be a cooperative one, with common goals and a mutual commitment to the ongoing spiritual nurturing of each other's members. The Church is the family of God, and the family needs to be a reflection of the nature of the kingdom of God.

When Jesus calls the Church to be the witness of the kingdom of God in Mark 3:31-35, it appears that Jesus doesn't value the family. On the contrary, Jesus redefines family by placing its top priority on seeking God. Likewise, as the Church seeks God, it develops an understanding of what it means to love each other as family. As this occurs, the *family of God* arrives at a better understanding of what it actually means to be family.

Counting on one another's presence and support—this is the heart of community. Families badly need this kind of community of extended family, friends, religious fellowships, neighborhoods, school groups, and other social organizations.

William J. Doherty, Ph.D.
The Intentional Family, 132-33

The power of the relationship between the family of God and the biological family is realized in the transformation of the lives of those who have no biological family in the church. When there are family members who aren't Christians (for example, fathers or mothers), members of the church can become surrogates for those relationships. For instance, men and women of the church can become *spiritual* fathers and mothers—and even grandparents—for the teens. In God's family, a childless couple has many children, and many parentless children have parents. Together they're members of the largest family the world has ever seen!

God's plan for His people is wholeness. To be whole, people need to develop physically, mentally, emotionally, socially, morally, and spiritually. A ministry to families with teens can be a means of God's grace that brings the family and its members to wholeness, as well as holiness.

This is only a bit of the story of how God wants to work with and through family. The story of the family is continually being written by those who seek to live out God's will in their own family. What a privilege you, as a youth worker, have in being able to minister to the family unit throughout this critical process!

── Family Strategy Builder ──

Now that we've looked at what the Bible says about family, it's time to conduct the first Family Strategy Builder. These activities will assist you as you begin developing your strategy for ministering to families with teens.

You may want to create a separate notebook or journal or computer file to help organize your research in these areas. These references will be invaluable to you in the future as you pray and dream about the role your ministry can play in the on-going development of the families in your church.

The first exercise below might take some time, so start it now and complete it as you continue with the rest of this book.

Not all the scriptures that talk about family were discussed in this chapter. Search for additional scriptures that relate to family. Here's a short list to get you started: Genesis 1:27-28, 31; 2 Samuel 5:1; 2 Samuel 19:12-13; Proverbs 1:8; 1 Corinthians 7:12-16; Ephesians 5:22—6:4; 1 Timothy 4:1-5; and 1 Peter 3. Again, this isn't a comprehensive listing, so continue searching the Bible for more references!

How do these scriptures deal with issues such as marriage, divorce and remarriage, adoption, foster parenting, dating, singleness, and senior adults? How do they complement a ministry to families with teens? You may want to use commentaries to gain a better understanding of the context and interpretation of some of the passages you'll discover. Remember, this will be an ongoing process, so you may want to add to your list as you continue developing your strategy.

Describe what it means to be a *spiritual* father or mother. Can you think of examples of where this is already happening in your church? Begin to list people in your church who are in need of these kinds of relationships. Think about how you can help connect them with *spiritual* fathers or mothers who can fulfill these roles.

chapter two

DEFINING THE FAMILY

*N*ow that we've reviewed the origins and biblical foundation for *family,* let's examine *(a)* how the family has evolved, *(b)* how a family is intended to function, and *(c)* how you and your youth ministry can help the family remain healthy and growing by working toward meeting its needs.

Family Evolution

What if you were to randomly survey a group of people for their definition of *family?* Chances are you'd collect a wide range of responses, representative of how the family and its various functions have evolved throughout time.

Some define family as a *traditional family* composed of a mom who stays at home, a dad who works outside of the home, 2.3 kids who mess up the home, and a dog that just messes. Some sources propose that fewer than 10 percent of the families in America can be considered as traditional according to this definition.

The U.S. government defines *family* as "a group of two or more persons related by birth, marriage, or adoption and residing together in a household."[2] But this definition doesn't always seem to work either. We all know people whom we consider family but yet don't fit these guidelines. What about noncustodial parents, aren't they family? Even our grandparents living across town can't be included as family according to the most technical interpretation of this definition.

Some define a *modern family* as a group of individuals who care deeply about one another. A biological relationship no longer automatically guarantees you a connection to the family. Instead, the status and privilege of family has to be earned. From this perspective, close friends can be considered family, while absent parents may be excluded from family status.

The biblical understanding of family is more than just units of people who pull into our church parking lots in the same vehicle. We are the *family of God,* and this family includes everyone in the Church—no matter how different, no matter what race or culture, no matter what social status or background. We're all from the same Creator, and we're in this family together. To take this understanding to its extreme, even those persons who aren't believers are members of the *family of God;* they just might be "prodigals" or "runaways." The family of God is an inclusive group, and all persons should know that they are valued and that they belong.

So, what *is* a family? Is there a single, working definition that we can use in our discussions regarding this issue? Maybe not. Everyone seems to have his or her own answer. And that's because everyone's history and situation is different.

Families come in many shapes and sizes: single-parent, dual-earner, traditional, blended, divorced, adoptive, foster, widowed, intergenerational, and so on. No one can pretend to know everything about families, and we should probably discontinue our search for a comprehensive, all-encompassing blueprint that fits all families. Instead, let's concentrate on learning how we can adapt our ministry efforts to intentionally minister to the varying needs that exist.

We now have the first society in human history without a clear social consensus about what constitutes a "real" family and "good" family. And I don't see one emerging anytime soon.

William J. Doherty, Ph.D.
The Intentional Family, 6

Essentially, what can be said concerning families is this: they exist in our churches; they have identifiable needs; and we're called to minister to them.

Family Functions

Since we can no longer diagram a typical family, let's look at how the family functions—no matter what its makeup. According to Dr. Charles Sell, professor of Christian education at Trinity Evangelical School and author of *Family Ministry,* the primary task of the family is to "individuate" its members.[3] Dr. Ed Robinson, dean of faculty and professor of Christian education at Nazarene Theological Seminary, explains this "individuation" process as parents committing to provide their teens with "roots and wings."

"Roots" pass along to a teen a sense of heritage and connectedness with his or her family. "Wings" offer a teen the ability and the confidence to be an individual apart from the family. If parents focus on only one aspect of this individuation process, dysfunction occurs. If the focus is on "roots," the family becomes enmeshed and the teen lacks autonomy. If parents concentrate too much on creating "wings," the family becomes disengaged and the teen lacks an identity. A balance between "roots" and "wings" is the goal that allows a teen to mature into an individual who is at the same time both connected and autonomous.

According to Sell, the major social functions a family serves include:

- *reproduction,*
- *sexual expression,*
- *socialization,*
- *status,*
- *economic cooperation,*
- *emotional satisfaction,* and
- *social control.*[4]

As we noted earlier, in order to be whole a person needs to develop physically, mentally, emotionally, socially, morally, and spiritually. So how does a family complete this list and help facilitate the development? Ideally, a family nurtures identity, defines boundaries, provides a sense of safety, and offers security to its members.

Developing Strong Families

Well, now that we've taken into account how families *should* operate, let's consider what families need in order to remain healthy and growing. While families are extremely diverse, there are some common denominators among strong families. According to a study of 3,000 families, the family unit is stronger when the members:

1. *are committed to the family;*
2. *spend time together;*
3. *have good family communication;*
4. *express appreciation to each other;*
5. *have a spiritual commitment; and*
6. *are able to solve problems in a crisis.*[5]

Charles Sell adds to this list the family's ability:

- *to negotiate changes in rules and roles,*
- *to handle changes in the amount and ways of showing affection,*
- *to foster a balance between independence and belonging, and*
- *to teach money management.*[6]

> *Y*ou are a human being first, and those human connections—with spouses, with children, with friends—are the most important investments you will ever make. At the end of your life . . . you will regret time not spent with a husband, a child, a friend, or a parent. . . . Our success as a society depends not on what happens in the White House but on what happens inside your house.
>
> Former First Lady Barbara Bu
> addressing graduating seniors from Wellesley Colle

A ministry to families with teens needs to assist families in becoming *strong* families. By planning activities through which parents and teens can interact in new and different ways, your youth ministry can be *the place* where families are strengthened. When you have recreational/game times for parents and teens, you help the family spend time together, communicate with each other, solve problems, and show appreciation and affection. Through seminars parents can come to a better understanding of how to adjust the roles and rules of their growing teen; understand their teen's growing need for freedom in addition to the continuing need for parental attachment and security; and learn how to help their teen manage money. By addressing the true needs of families, we can do more than just hand out Band-Aids. We can help avoid future eruptions by meeting needs before the families reach a crisis point.

> *As the family goes, so goes the nation, and so goes the whole world in which we live.*
>
> Pope John Paul II

The strength and stability of the church depend on the strength and stability of its families. Thus, the stronger the families, the stronger the church. The church cannot focus solely on meeting the spiritual needs of families. The church needs to also address the physical, mental, emotional, social, and moral needs of families.

⎯⎯ Family Strategy Builder ⎯⎯

So, do you know what a family is and how it's supposed to work? Hopefully, you now have a better idea of where your ministry is headed! These questions will help you apply the previous material to your local church setting. This exercise will also help you further develop your strategy of ministry to families with teens. Complete the following questions before moving on to the next section.

How do you define family? How do you determine who's in your own family? Who are the members of your family?

Think of the families represented in your youth ministry. What are the different types of families to which you minister? Consider all the various examples: traditional, divorced, single-parent, blended, widowed, etc.

Reflect on the unique family contexts represented by each type of family. What are some specific needs of these families? Of individual family members? What are you doing to address these needs? How can you improve the effectiveness of your ministry in these areas?

Review the ways a family is meant to function in the ongoing development of its members. How well are the families you're ministering to functioning? How can you assist them in becoming stronger, healthier families?

chapter three:

MODELS OF FAMILY MINISTRY

A few years ago the first family-based youth ministry books and articles started rolling off the presses. The primary reason for this boom wasn't that ministry to families with teens wasn't taking place, but rather the interest grew from the realization that as youth workers, we are simply not the most influential persons in our teens' lives.

Examples of excellent and thriving youth ministries were plentiful, but at the same time, we youth workers often struggled to identify cases where our ministry efforts could be seen making long-term differences in the lives of our youth. Our ministry efforts seemed compartmentalized. As youth workers, we had access to our kids at certain times for a limited number of years. Outside of those parameters, we had few opportunities to minister to a teen. Were we ultimately wasting our time?

Eventually, youth ministry realized that something needed to be done. But what? One response was to broaden our ministry focus to include our teens' families. Youth ministries across denominational lines have seen this approach add both effectiveness and efficiency to their efforts. By encouraging, empowering, and equipping parents, youth workers now are helping *parents* nurture their teens' spiritual needs. As this happens, we begin to work *with* families rather than *against* them, no longer competing with each other.

But a new problem has arisen. It's essentially a mixed blessing, confirming for us that ministering to families in the context of youth ministry is an important and viable ministry. It's a situation that has flooded our office voice mail and E-mail—especially since the 1996 publication of *101 Ways to Be Family-Friendly in Youth Ministry.* Here's how the typical story goes:

Ring . . . ring. "Hi, this is Mike. May I help you?"

"Hi, I'm a youth worker, and I need some help. I know I need to do more in the area of 'family ministry,' but I have absolutely no idea where to begin! Exactly what does 'ministry to families with teens' mean—I'm a youth minister, not a family counselor! What's this mean for my current youth ministry? Will I need to totally revamp my program? And there's no way I can do this by myself—how do I sell this concept to my pastor and youth staff? To the families themselves? I know I need to do something . . . but where do I start?"

The questions come in various voices and formats and from many different youth ministry settings, but they're all essentially saying the same thing: *How do I take my current youth ministry from where it is to where it needs to be?*

The "Family Ministry" Market

Many have relied on a few resources to explain what family ministry might look like in a youth ministry context. In the May/June 1996 issue of *Group* magazine, Dave Rahn published the article "Parafamily Youth Ministry," which outlined four different models for combining family and youth ministry. And in 1997, Chap Clark offered his organizing principle of what family ministry looks like in his most recent book, *The Youth Worker's Handbook to Family Ministry.*

Rahn describes four narrowly defined models of family ministry. Each model is based upon the focus of the ministry and the level of the parents' involvement. Each model can be weighed by measuring the parents' role and the church's role in the spiritual nurture of teens. A perceived increase in the parents' role is countered by a decrease in the church's role as the primary spiritual nurturer, and vice versa. Rahn's four models are "Family-Friendly Youth Ministry," "Family-Focused Youth Ministry," "Youth-Focused Family Ministry," and "Youth-Friendly Family Ministry."

Clark identifies three perspectives a church may choose to adopt—all of which are less programmatic than those Rahn describes: "Counseling-Therapeutic Focus," "Focus on the Nuclear Family," and "The Church as Family." Each perspective is distinguished by the role the church plays in the spiritual discipling process of its youth. Family ministry is best achieved, Clark states, when it functions from a balance of these three guiding perspectives.

Let's examine these seven philosophies to discover if any of these methods will work for your youth ministry.

Family-Friendly Youth Ministry / This method assumes a traditional approach to youth ministry while at the same time encouraging youth workers to be sensitive to the needs of the family. Parents are minimally involved in the youth ministry, but the youth ministry places no additional burden on families. Activities are geared toward youth, again keeping the family in mind. The church staff remains as the main nurturers of the teens' faith. Tangible examples of a family-friendly youth ministry include scheduling meals before services; planning youth activities so that they don't conflict with school, the holidays, and other family commitments; and using creative fund-raising to keep activity expenses low. This model accommodates the needs of the family but still keeps the reins of spiritual nurture ultimately in the hands of the youth worker.

Family-Focused Youth Ministry / Rahn calls this model the slash approach because of the "/" included in the titles of many youth group activities. Examples of "slash" events include a father/daughter date or a mother/son role reversal night. It could even include a communication workshop for big siblings/little siblings. These programs target both teens and their parents, but the responsibility for spiritual nurturing still lies with the youth worker. This model does, however, increase the amount of influence the youth worker has on the family, primarily through increased interaction with family members. One of the main critiques of this model is that outreach to unchurched teens and families is less likely to take place since the "slash programs" are geared toward families with at least one member being associated with the church.

Youth-Focused Family Ministry / This approach helps empower and equip parents with the tools and skills necessary to better nurture their teens. In this model, the reins of spiritual nurture are handed over to the parents and the youth worker is viewed more as a resource—the "youth specialist." The parents determine the direction of the ministry by their felt needs, and the youth worker equips them to do ministry. Equipping is not done to rob parents of their responsibility but rather to empower them. This ministry might involve starting a parent support group, starting a parent newsletter, or organizing a mission trip that includes both teens and parents. Obviously, in this model the parents' role has greatly increased, and the church's role has decreased.

Youth-Friendly Family Ministry / According to Rahn's final model, the family is the top priority. The focus of ministry here is the family and the equipping of the parents to minister to their teens. Traditional youth-only events are acceptable, but they are seen as secondary to family activities. Activities are focused on the family, since the more grounded the family is in its faith, the stronger the teens will be in theirs. The church is seen as a resource for family life education, including helping the family do Christian education in the home. Programs such as a small-group ministry (where families mentor one another) and seminars on family issues are examples of this model.

Counseling-Therapeutic Focus / The first of Clark's three perspectives involves what he calls guardrails and medical centers. In this ministry model, the church provides people, programs, and opportunities for healing and help. Many churches today are beginning to open in-church counseling centers as a ministry to church members, as well as the community. Clark terms these "medical centers." Many churches also offer educational programs as the preventive arm of the church to families and the community; Clark has coined these "guardrails."

Two downsides to this approach exist, however. First, no matter how good the guardrail programs are, they only reach a small portion of the people in a congregation and community. In

most cases, the only families who attend these educational programs are the families in the churches and communities that
truly need them the least. Second, sometimes these guardrails
are built on roads where no family is traveling—either the seminars don't relate to actual needs or they're totally outdated.

The positive side of this approach is that it proactively at-
tempts to help parents. Through counseling, a family facing a
crisis can receive the therapeutic help that often contributes to
growth and healing in relationships.

Focus on the Nuclear Family / This approach targets the
nuclear family as the main discipling agent for children. It
deemphasizes the various age-level ministries by instead
equipping parents to nurture faith in their children. The downside of this perspective is that it only works for those families
who are (1) truly nuclear and (2) confident in their abilities to
disciple their own children. As we've already seen, the traditional nuclear family is a distinct minority of our current popu-
lation. Add to this the fact that most parents feel inadequate in
their own faith—let alone their ability to disciple their teens—
and the number of families affected by this approach is greatly
reduced.

Church as Family / Clark's third perspective of family
ministry is what he calls the best New Testament expression of
the local church. The "Church as Family" perspective strength-
ens and supports parents to raise their children in a household
that serves the Lord. This model broadly defines family ministry so that the church community itself becomes like an extended family. Where the family is weak, the extended family
of the church provides support and assistance. When a parent
is unable to disciple a teen, for whatever reason, the church
fulfills the obligation.

The downside of this model is an overemphasis on community life, with a disregard for the needs of individual families—potentially causing more harm than good to the family
system. When the family has to be in competition with the
church for the limited free time of its teens, the family often
loses. And when the family loses, the loss always reflects itself
back upon the overall health of the church community.

Clark offers some further advice on these three models. If a
church focuses solely on one of the three perspectives without

including the essential elements of the other two, Clark believes the church will always lose out in the end. He suggests that churches maintain a balanced combination of all three approaches. Every church, Clark says, should *(a)* have a counseling or pastoral care ministry, *(b)* minister to the needs and issues of the nuclear family, and *(c)* view itself as being the family of God. He further notes that every church must answer three questions before it begins a family ministry: What are the needs of the people? How does the church's theology fit the needs? What resources are available to meet the needs?

So What's the Answer?

Which approach should have priority? Each model seems to have certain advantages and disadvantages, potential benefits and possible drawbacks. Left to these choices, what's a youth worker to do? Are any of these approaches the "answer," or is there something else out there somewhere that will better meet your needs?

So the question is no longer as simple as "What's the best way to minister to my teens and their families?" Rather, your search now includes considerations such as "Is my youth ministry contributing positively toward the health of the family?" "Am I working with, or against, my teens' parents?" "How can my youth ministry achieve its goals but also better equip the families of my teens to achieve their goals as well?"

My personal experience and involvement with these questions has led me to believe that the most effective approach you can take to youth ministry in your local church setting is through developing a "ministry to families with teens." We've examined what others have suggested regarding family ministry. A "ministry to families with teens" isn't an altogether new philosophy; instead, this perspective combines some elements from existing models in a way that provides both the *balance* and *intentionality* that are necessary to the success of your youth ministry.

Keep It Balanced!

A ministry to families with teens does alter the framework of your youth ministry, requiring it to be more inclusive of the family. It doesn't mean we never spend time with or provide programs for teens apart from their families. Developmentally, though, teens are in the process of *becoming,* and they are searching for examples of who they need to become. By connecting teens with Christian parents and other adults in the church, your teens are placed into direct contact with Christian role models who can help them become Christian adults. When a teen's parents aren't examples of Christian adults, other Christian adults in the church need to fill that role. Know this for a fact: If such a void exists, and if the church is not able to connect these teens with appropriate adult role models, the world is more than ready to step in. Your youth ministry needs to be a place where families, and the church community, come together to be the family of God.

If we do not teach our children, society will. And they—and we—will live with the results.

Stephen R. Covey
The Seven Habits of Highly Effective Families, 146

But teens also need time to be apart from their parents, times where they're allowed to begin developing their own sense of independence. Youth ministry needs to continue fostering an environment where teens are allowed to be teens and not prematurely forced to be adults. Sure, they'll goof up, slip up, and fall down in their faith. Your youth ministry should be there as they learn how to get back up. The church needs to be a place where teens can test their "wings" in a safe environment.

Be Intentional!

Take a moment to examine your youth ministry. You may already be ministering to families with teens to some extent. You probably hold a parents' meeting a couple times a year to keep the parents up-to-date with what's happening in your youth ministry. At one time or another you've had to discuss a problem with a teen's parent to

We now live in the best and worst of times for families. The worst of times because . . . the community and culture are unable to provide a coherent vision or set of tools and supports. . . . The best of times because we understand better what makes families work.

William J. Doherty, Ph.D.
The Intentional Family, 6

better understand the underlying circumstances behind a situation.

You probably talk with parents when they drop their teens off or pick them up from youth events. Maybe you've asked some parents to help prepare breakfast for the youth after an all-nighter. Possibly, a family has invited you over for a meal, or maybe some families have been willing to sponsor after-church youth fellowships in their homes. Perhaps a few parents have even joined your youth ministry staff as youth sponsors. If any of these scenarios fit you, guess what! You're already "doing" ministry to families with teens!

Before you get too comfortable, however, you still need to address the issue of intentionality. How much, if any, of your current involvement with the family beyond the individual teen has been initiated *by you?* How purposefully have you sought out and planned times and activities that would naturally encourage participation from parents? How content have you been to just let these moments happen on their own?

By increasing your intentionality, you can have a greater influence on teens and their families. Since the parent is the most influential person in a teen's life, the more you equip parents to disciple their teen, the greater the impact of the discipleship. The more *you* plan for parents to be involved with their teen, the more likely *they* will be to continue that pattern. Our society tries to pull parents and teens apart; your youth ministry can be a place to bring them together.

Families don't get together merely by accident; it almost always has to be planned. The church can help families learn to mold the ordinary aspects of family life into opportunities for teaching the faith. And churches can support, equip, and release families as witnesses in the homes, businesses, and schools where these church families live, work, and learn every day.

Reach Out, Reach In!

The approaches to family ministry proposed earlier by Clark and Rahn neglected to focus sufficiently on two areas that are significantly affected when family ministry is introduced to a youth ministry: *evangelism* and *discipleship.* At its core, youth ministry should reflect the basic tenets of the New Testament church, and two of the Early Church's main emphases were evangelism and discipleship. You can already see this pattern worked out in the everyday life of your youth group as activities and ministry efforts focus on reaching out to teens on the fringes of the youth group (evangelism) and to those teens who form your core group (discipleship).

Your youth ministry should assist the parents of your teens in achieving these goals within their family settings. A major feature of ministering to families with teens is assisting parents in discipling their teens in the Christian faith. One of the most powerful positive influences upon a teen's behavior is involvement with family in spiritual activities and discussions.[7] In families where the parents and teens attend church together, pray together, read the Bible together, and openly talk about their faith on a regular basis, teens are found to be more positive and more likely to volunteer and to engage individually in various forms of religious activity [i.e., praying daily, reading the Bible daily, attending a church group each week, attending weekly Bible studies, attending Sunday School].[8] Ministry to families with teens aims to assist and equip parents in fulfilling the task assigned to them in Ephesians 6:4, to be Christian parents, a responsibility that includes the nurturing of their teens in the faith.

The key to evangelism in a ministry to families with teens is the approach. People are more responsive to the claims of the gospel when they believe that the church is genuinely concerned about the individual needs of their family. They appreciate a church that is willing to demonstrate its faith by acknowledging their struggles and by helping them learn how to improve their family relationships.

By functioning as an outreach arm of the church, a ministry to families with teens can be a method of making faith

> *A*s families feel loved, supported, and encouraged, their faith will become more practical and meaningful. Whatever strategies the church adopts for strengthening families, its investment of resources will pay rich dividends in terms of both family stability and church growth.
>
> Jim Larson
> *A Church Guide for Strengthening Families*, 24

come alive through action. Nonchurch families will have opportunities to experience the church through marriage conferences, parenting classes, counseling services, or other seminars. Training for parents in the areas of child development, counseling, relationships, problem-solving skills, financial planning, communication, and parenting skills can serve as an extremely effective outreach tool of the church.

A ministry to families with teens ultimately reflects an understanding of the goals of the New Testament church. Through your involvement, families can reinforce and restore their relationships and can nurture each other in their faith journeys. And as families enrich the quality of their lives together, the Body of Christ—your church—is strengthened in the process.

────── Family Strategy Builder ──────

There are many different models for you to choose from as you begin tailor-making your "ministry to families with teens." To help you determine what your ministry to families with teens will look like, ask yourself the following questions to assist in developing your personal strategy. After completing these questions, you'll be ready to begin implementing your ministry to families with teens.

What do *you* see as the pros and cons of the various models of family ministry described in this chapter? Which best describes your youth ministry now? What portions of each model best describe what you would like your ministry to become?

Which elements of your current youth ministry could be improved with participation from parents and families? What youth-only programs can you eliminate and replace (or adapt) with programming designed for the whole family? How are you building bridges to parents?

Are you achieving the ministry goals of evangelism and discipleship in your youth ministry? What are you doing now to equip parents to disciple their teens? How can you adapt your youth ministry to better help parents meet these goals?

Part two

To Raise a Youth Ministry

I'd like to suggest that in everything you do in your family, you keep in mind the miracle of the Chinese bamboo tree. After the seed for this amazing tree is planted, you see nothing—absolutely nothing for four years except a tiny shoot coming out of a bulb. During those four years, all the growth is underground in a massive, fibrous root structure that spreads deep and wide in the earth. But then in the fifth year the Chinese bamboo tree grows up to 80 feet!

Many things in family life are like the Chinese bamboo tree. You work, and you invest time and effort, and you do everything you can possibly do to nurture growth, and sometimes you don't see anything for weeks, months, or even years. But if you're patient and keep working and nurturing, that "fifth year" will come, and you will be astonished at the growth and change you see taking place.

—Stephen R. Covey
The Seven Habits of Highly Effective Families

Youth ministry cannot be healthy if it is isolated from the family. Careful attention to strategy is needed to maximize the valuable role parents play as partners in helping their kids reach their spiritual potential. While neither students nor parents inherently want total integration, there are some deliberate ways to build a family-friendly youth ministry.

—Doug Fields—
Purpose Driven Youth Ministry

It's a Marathon, Not a Sprint

*S*o far, we've examined what the Bible says about family and relationships; we've reviewed the family's definition, role, and function; and we've looked at suggestions for ministering to families with teens. Your responses to the Family Strategy Builders in part 1 will form the basis of your "ministry to families with teens" philosophy. Take some time now to review your journal notes.

It's time to put this philosophy into action. Your approach will be tailored to fit your existing youth ministry and can be implemented at just the right pace for your families and teens. This is where the "rubber meets the road." Putting your philosophy into action can be done in just five easy steps.

Five steps to a ministry to families with teens:

- *Survey* the needs of the families in your church and community.
- *Review* your resources to see what you have available.
- *Develop* a plan of action to connect these needs and resources together in new ways.
- *Follow* the plan of action as you minister to families with teens. And remember to pace yourself!
- *Evaluate* your ministry to be sure you are meeting the needs of those in your church and community.

As you develop your ministry to families with teens, you'll need to see it as more than a *program for* ministry. It is an *attitude of* ministry. Part of this attitude is understanding that ministry to families with teens occurs in both formal and informal settings (i.e., Sunday School classes, worship services, parent meetings, family date nights, family game nights, going to sporting events, etc.).

As we explore the transition from where you're at currently to a thriving, functional ministry to families with teens, we can compare it to the training of distance runners. Runners don't just wake up one day and run a race. There's a lot of work that takes place before race day. Runners are always training and conditioning. They set goals. They eat the right food, drink the right drinks. Runners work toward building up their endurance. They stretch and warm up before they run. Running isn't easy work—it takes a commitment, it takes endurance, and it takes getting off on the right foot.

Generally, the training goes somewhat unnoticed by others. The training you have completed so far may also go unnoticed. But, just like the runner, the work you've put in will pay off in the long run. The training will give you endurance, an indispensable attribute when the race gets tough.

chapter four

ON YOUR MARK

*H*ave you ever noticed how much time runners take in positioning themselves on the starting line? Sometimes it seems like forever. They're extremely focused and deliberate. They make sure everything is just right. These athletes have learned what's necessary to ensure a good start and how important their start is to running the race. A bad start leads to a rough race that ends with a poor finish. Getting started well is crucial to running a good race, not to mention winning!

Do you see where we're going here? As you prepare to begin this new phase in your ministry, you'll need to concentrate on developing a good "starting mind-set," on positioning your youth ministry where it needs to be to get started, and on knowing what needs to be in place to ensure your "race" begins well.

And remember: most runners don't approach the race alone—they have coaches and trainers and fans cheering them along the way. Before you start *your* race, gather your "fans." Some of your strongest supporters will be your senior pastor, other church staff members, the church board, and other leaders in your church. Their support will help get you started on the right foot. Share with them your vision for ministering to families with teens. Allow them to see why you believe this is important for your youth ministry, as well as for the church in general. A spirit of cooperation and involvement from others will show that this ministry is connected to the other church ministries.

Surveying the Landscape

As you approach the starting line, you'll want to "survey the course"—the families with teens in your church and community. A survey will help you map out the route you and your ministry will be taking in the months and years to come. Surveying your families with teens will help you see the areas on which your ministry will need to focus. This step is critically important—as a runner, you need to know what lies before you.

Special attention needs to be given to surveying. By surveying the families, you will discover areas where families feel they could use the church's assistance. Part 3 contains a sample of a family survey that you can use or adapt to survey the families with teens in your church and community. The information you'll gather will help you shape your ministry to families with teens. The survey will take you at least two to three weeks to finish, so begin the survey as soon as possible. Feel free to move on to chapter 5 while you're completing this project.

Getting Ready to Run

Gather a committee of 8 to 12 people—including both parents and teens and those from a variety of family situations. These people should represent a wide range of backgrounds, talents, and needs. The family survey and your ministry philosophy will help give direction to this committee. Together, you will map out the course you will all run.

Once you have your committee selected, there are several tasks you'll need to accomplish. The first will be to analyze the information from the survey to find out the needs that are noted. These needs will help you see what your church can do to meet the needs of its people.

The words of Jesus, "Be as shrewd as snakes and innocent as doves," aptly describe the ideal members of a family ministry committee. So look for people who are not only influential, but godly and gentle as well. If the members of the committee are godly but relationally meek, they will be fun to work with but may not accomplish much.

Chap Clark
*The Youth Worker's Handbook
to Family Ministry, 48*

The next step is to look at the different resources and programs your church currently has, or should have, in order to meet the identified needs. (At this point, dream a little. Pretend you're in a perfect world without any limitations. Anything goes!) An example might be that your survey noted that communication in the home is a problem and that some people could benefit from a seminar on parent/teen communication or from some family counseling in this area. Maybe your church already knows a Christian counselor to whom you refer people when a counseling need arises. Find out from the counselor whether he or she would be open to conducting seminars on communication in your church. If so, then you've been able to effectively match an available resource (a willing professional) with an existing need (the desire for assistance with family communication issues). This same process can be followed for each need identified in the survey.

An Organized Approach

After making a list of the needs and resources, try to group the items into four categories. This organization will help you balance your ministry. The first category is **Family Support.** This category is similar to Chap Clark's medical centers and guardrails. It's the area of your ministry where emotionally driven needs are addressed. Resources such as counseling, crisis intervention, emergency relief, and support groups are examples of some of the resources that are found in this category.

Family Education is the second category. This is the arm of your ministry that *teaches* different aspects of how to be a Christian family. These teaching opportunities take place in various settings such as weekend retreats, Sunday School classes, and seminars. Topics that can easily be covered in these retreats, classes, and seminars include growing deeper in one's faith; a Christian view toward sex and sexuality; helping family members relate to one another; improving communication in the family; and developing planning skills for the future, fun, and finances.

The third category is **Family Enrichment.** This is the arm of your ministry that helps families improve their relationships by being proactive in planning and scheduling their time and activities. One major part of this is deprogramming the church's ministries so the family is not being pulled apart for more than three nights a week. Another area of this category is looking at the current church programming to see how you can help bring families together for better interaction in church. A great example of this is the traditional potluck dinner after church or an organized time of family worship. Family enrichment also includes providing opportunities for families to relax, play, and have fun together. Family game nights and outings would certainly fall into this category. Finally, this category also provides the family with opportunities to serve others together through outlets such as family service projects and mission trips.

The final category is **Family Outreach.** This is the arm of your ministry that equips the family to reach out to other families in your community. This can be done through publicizing those seminars, retreats, and classes that meet the felt needs of people whether they are Christians or not. Generally, when people believe that the church is able to meet their felt needs (emotional, social, or physical), they're more open to allow the church to attend to their spiritual needs as well.

You Can't Do It All: Prioritize!

Once your needs and resources have been categorized, evaluate how balanced your ministry is currently. You'll most likely notice some areas that you're doing too much in and others you may need to do more in. You will need to prioritize what you can do. No church can do everything and meet every need. You cannot assume a shotgun approach and be effective. Instead, focus in on a few needs that you can effectively meet, and pursue them. Your committee should discuss what they feel God's calling is for this ministry, which are the greatest needs of the people, and what would be the best use of available resources—including time.

Setting Goals and Objectives

Now it's time for your committee to form a mission statement for your church's ministry to families with teens. The most effective mission statements are brief and concise—primarily because they're then easier to remember and keep in the forefront of your thinking at all times. Make sure the statement correctly summarizes the purpose and focus of your ministry. You might want to review the existing mission statements of your church and your youth ministry so that the mission statement you're creating for your ministry to families with teens will support those mission statements as well. Remember: A mission statement needs to be comprehensive (but concise), easy to understand and remember, and shared by everyone involved.

To accomplish this, have each committee member write his or her own mission statement proposal. Have each person read his or her proposal aloud to the committee. Make notes of common themes, words, and phrases. Then begin to create one mission statement that reflects the corporate thoughts of the committee. (An example of a mission statement might be: "Our church seeks to build bridges between parents and teens by edifying, enriching, educating, and evangelizing families for the sake of the gospel.")

After you've settled on a mission statement, it's time to begin looking at what format your new ministry will take. It's time to develop your objectives—the goals you want to accomplish and the criteria you will use to evaluate the effectiveness of programs and activities. Some possible goals might be to help parents and teens communicate better, to help parents disciple their teens, or to help parents and teens have fun together. Some objectives that fit these goals might be holding a parent/teen communication seminar, starting parent/teen Bible studies, and planning parent/teen recreation nights at the church.

Thus far, you've been dreaming somewhat in a "perfect world" setting. In order for your objectives to be real, however, it's time to consider any potential limitations you might have to deal with. Limitations usually come in three varieties. The first is **leadership.** Who's going to lead the program(s) and activities? It is best to present the mission statement of the committee to the congregation and then allow God to raise up people to coordinate certain programs. If a person doesn't feel called to lead a program, then he or she probably won't give it the energy and passion it requires.

The second limitation is **facilities.** Make good use of the buildings you have, but continue to dream of what you want.

Think creatively. Many schools rent their gymnasiums or auditoriums. Utilize state parks. Rent another church's gym or classrooms.

Oh, and finally, there's **money.** (You knew this was coming, didn't you?) You need to estimate well the financial implications of any potential activity or program. Think about how much the other two limitations are going to cost you. Are you bringing in a special speaker? Do you need to rent space? Are you traveling somewhere? Will you need to provide childcare for participants? Be realistic, yes; but be creative as well. You can build these expenses into the cost of the activity, pay for them out of an existing budget, or solicit donations to your ministry. (Remember: some professionals will speak at classes and seminars at no charge if you allow them to also promote their vocation.)

Following this chapter's Family Strategy Builder, we've included an easy-to-use form for your committee to utilize in identifying areas of ministry, existing needs, available resources, additional resources necessary, and objectives and limitations for each activity/program. Use this chart as a guide to examine the issues your surveys indicate are important to the parents and teens in your church and community. The example provided deals with helping families spend more time together.

——— Family Strategy Builder ———

Use the results from your family survey (in part 3) to answer the following questions.

What needs do the surveyed families list? What needs can you meet, and which do you need to refer to others who are better trained (e.g., counseling, crisis management, etc.)? Make a list of ways to meet those needs. If your church doesn't have a counselor on staff, or if you don't know of a Christian counselor, a guide to help you find one is included in part 3 of this book.

What types of activities and events do you anticipate in your ministry to families with teens? How many events and activities will focus on just the parents? the teens? the whole family?

In what ways can other church leaders contribute from their various areas of ministry?

Programming Form Example

Area of Ministry	Need Addressed	Available Resources	Objective	Limitation
Enriching Family Life	Help families spend more time together.	101 Ways to Be Family-Friendly in Youth Ministry, Lytle, Schwartz, Hartke. Beacon Hill Press of Kansas City, 1996 (083-411-6596).	Reevaluate current programming to see how we separate families. (By April 15)	Who will lead the activity?
			Begin a monthly church activity for families of teens. (By June 15)	How much will it cost?
				Where will it be held?
				Is day care needed?

chapter five

GET SET

*A*sk runners and they'll probably tell you that some of the longest stretches of time seem to be those few seconds just after the starter yells, "Get set!" Time seems to stand still while the runner anticipates the sound of the starting gun. Let's do the same. There are a couple of important items that need to be addressed before your race starts.

Have you wondered why some people may train well for a race and yet don't perform well on the big day? Maybe their concentration wasn't what it needed to be at that moment, or maybe they were distracted by other issues in their lives. Maybe they were unable to make adjustments to obstacles such as sore muscles or dehydration. To help *you* run the best race you can, let's take a look at some obstacles you might face during your upcoming race.

Change

If there's one thing people tend to resist, it's change. With this in mind, remember that you can't force anyone to change—a person has to *want* to change before anything can happen. Usually, people have to believe there's a real need for change before they will be supportive of the impending change. You need to wait until the timing is right to introduce the change.

You might discover that change is not only tough for those affected by the transition—but also tough for those who are leading and coordinating the change process. It's easy to avoid change altogether; the status quo is comfortable. But God doesn't call His people to an environment of continual comfort. He calls us to a lifetime of continual improvement, and He has promised to guide us in these changes. Change may be your first obstacle to overcome, but with God's help—and with plenty of prayer and preparation—you will make it through!

Communication

Communicating is tricky business and can be a significant obstacle. Have you ever played the game where you whisper a secret in someone's ear, and that person whispers it to the next person, and so on, until the secret has traveled through 10 or 15 people. Almost every time, what the last person says he or she heard is totally different from the original secret! This type of miscommunication can easily happen in your youth ministry if steps aren't taken to ensure that your communication methods are clear, concise, and consistent.

If we are secretive about the youth ministry or the program, parents will get suspicious. We must let them know what's happening in the youth group. We also must communicate to parents that we are willing to listen to them; ignoring their wisdom and experience will cause us to sacrifice a great many insights.

Paul Borthwick
Organizing Your Youth Ministry, 193

Have you ever said something in a youth group meeting and had a teen go home and tell his or her parents that you said something totally different? How good is your direct communication to parents? Do you send out letters or newsletters? Do you conduct meetings so parents know what you are doing? Or do you rely on your teens to pass along all the pertinent information? The better you communicate to the family, the fewer instances of miscommunication you'll experience. The more direct your communication with parents, the more likely they will hear what you really intend to be heard.

Fear

Another obstacle that some youth workers may face in ministering to families with teens is fear of the parents of your teens. Some youth workers have created their own obstacles. For example, have you ever come back late from a retreat? I mean *really* late—like three hours late! Some youth workers might have some past goof-ups that have hurt their credibility and essentially "burned the bridges" between themselves and parents. Other times in the hustle to "do" ministry, we unintentionally communicate to parents that they are in the way or aren't valuable to our youth ministry.

Parents can be your friends, and many times they will be your best supporters. But remember that you are asking parents to trust you with one of the most important things in their lives—their teenager! Don't betray this trust, certainly. But know that most parents *want* to partner with you in nurturing their teen's spiritual growth and maturity. Don't fear this often-untapped source of encouragement and support.

Professionalism

The manner with which you present yourself will shape how parents think about you. Don't try so hard to fit in with your teens that you lose the respect of your fellow ministry colleagues or church members. If you look like a teen, act like a teen, and talk like a teen, then you just might **be** a teen in their eyes. That doesn't mean you need to wear a suit and tie the next time you take the group out for pizza, but when you are with parents, it might be best to not act like a teen. Be yourself. This will help you relate to both teens and parents.

Knowing Your Role

Some people have said that the role of a youth worker is that of an advocate—a person who is neither a parent (even though you might be) nor a teen in the immediate environment of your youth ministry. As an advocate, you need to be an expert on teen culture to the parents *and* an expert on adult culture to your teens. Taking this neutral position enables you to talk to both teens and parents.

Although you may be looked at as an expert on the two cultures, you cannot know a teen better than his or her parents, nor a parent better than his or her teen. Few things will open a communication chasm between a youth worker and a parent faster than when a youth worker tells a father or mother that he or she knows a teen better than does the parent.

Maybe your relationship with parents is another obstacle you will need to overcome. There's no quick fix for the past—only what can happen in the present and the future. As parents see that you are truly concerned about their family's well-being, they will begin to see you in a different light. They may even forgive *and* forget the past. As you concentrate on positive family development and help parents disciple their teens, you will build bridges over the obstacles separating you and them.

Pace Yourself

Now you're set to start the race. Remember that the race you're about to run is a long race, so don't take off too fast. Be ready to make some adjustments along the way to avoid some obstacles. Don't try to fulfill all of the needs at once—give yourself time. Make your moves at the right time, and develop the ministry gradually. Begin slowly, pace yourself, and run for the long haul.

—— Family Strategy Builder ——

Now that we've considered several factors involved in building your ministry to families with teens and reviewed some obstacles you might face as you begin, let's take a time-out to continue developing this strategy. Complete the following questions before moving on to the next section. These questions will help you apply the previous material to your local church.

How are your relationships with the parents of your youth group? Have you burned any bridges that are in need of restoration? What are you doing to build, or rebuild, strong bridges of communication, support, and mutual encouragement?

2

What obstacles do you need to prepare for in your race? How do the parents in your church view you? What are you doing to influence the way you are viewed by parents?

3

How effectively do you communicate to the parents of your youth group? How frequently does miscommunication occur? What are you doing that promotes good communication between you and the parents in your group?

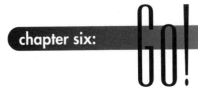

chapter six

*G*o!" The starting gun has sounded, and it's time to begin the race—time to start your ministry to families with teens. There may be adjustments to make in the midst of the race. You might even find a few unexpected obstacles, but thanks to your training, you will be ready for the obstacles as they appear. You will need to determine how fast you run this race and the exact course you'll take. We've provided you with some guidelines, but this is your race to run. And remember, not everybody's course will look the same—what works for some, might not work for everyone.

As you look at what programming options you will introduce to your ministry to families with teens, you may want to consider offering some activities that are the same each year in order to build tradition into the program. You also may want to offer some options that are different each year, adding variety to your ministry efforts. Be creative and stay fresh in how you program. Evaluate each element as you go—this will help measure your progress in "the race."

Presenting the Program

Your race should begin with having the family committee prepare a report. This report should include the reasons why a ministry to families with teens is needed, a report of support from the church leadership, the family survey results, the needs indicated, any resources available, and the plan of action developed by the family committee. This report will provide you with a framework for the presentation of your program to your church.

When you present your ministry proposal to your parents and teens, there are different ways you can accomplish this.

One way is to hold a parent/teen meeting after church on a Sunday night. Have the members of your family committee present. Involve them in presenting "the ministry to families with teens" program to the crowd gathered. Another way is less explicit. Sponsor a parent/teen game night (or other activity). After the games, have the committee's report available and give a short talk on the importance of the family and why ministering to families is so critical to your youth ministry.

The setting for your presentation is up to you. But however you do it, publicize your meeting—through the church bulletin, church newsletter, youth group newsletter, a letter to parents, flyers in the community, and so on. Act as if you're marketing the one thing that will revolutionize the world—*because you are!*

Don't give in to the illusion that all will sing your praises after the first event, because they may not. Don't even think that all the families with teens will participate in the first event; in fact, you might find that the majority of the families that do attend and participate will be the families that are already the strongest families in your youth ministry. Don't get frustrated— there's nothing wrong with making strong families even stronger! There may be some underlying issues that prevent some families from participating at first. But don't give up!

You may also notice that some of the teens in your youth group might not like the idea of their parents being involved. Reassure them that not every activity or event will include their parents, but that from time to time the parents will be involved. Over time the resistance will fade as the program grows more familiar to everyone and as more families with teens take advantage of this ministry.

Ministry vs. Programming

Speaking of ministry, we should probably explore the relationship between "ministry" and "programming" now before you get started. Ministry and programming are not adversaries; rather they work together to help you strengthen families and point them to Christ. Programming is how you meet the needs of people—it's *what* you do and *how* you do it. Ministry is the motive of the programming—*why* you do what you do. Anything you've been doing with teens alone can most likely be adapted to work with teens and parents together.

There are different categories of programming you should consider as you develop your program. The basic categories include worship, service, education, discipleship, evangelism, and recreation. A balance of programming in these areas is the best approach. Start by having one activity from each category your first year, and then add one or two activities in these categories in future years.

Worship / How involved are your teens in the worship services at your church? The more involved teens are in worship, the more they are positively affected by what they experience—and the better the long-term results. Teens' involvement in worship is extremely critical to their spiritual growth. Involvement provides a sense of belonging to the Church, inclusion in the family of God, and membership in His kingdom. Scripture readers, ushers, prayer leaders, singers, musicians, and greeters are just some of the different roles teens can fill to be intentionally involved in the worship experience.

Service / The church can also be a place where teens and adults serve side by side. By having teens involved in service to others, they learn how to be proactive and not reactive. When teens and Christian adults serve others together, teens also see adults living out their faith in real-life situations—and this helps nurture their faith. Since parents are the primary nurturers of their teens' faith, this type of involvement is especially effective when families can partner together in service opportunities.

Visiting a nursing home, building a Habitat for Humanity house, cleaning up a community park, cleaning and repairing the homes of the elderly, and doing yardwork for physically dependent individuals are just a few examples of service projects in which parents and teens can participate together. This is certainly not an exhaustive list, and you can probably think of many other similar options. Think of your youth group's last mission trip. How could your experience have benefited from the involvement of your teens' parents?

Education / How does your church educate its members? If it's anything like most churches, it's done in age-segregated classes. For the teens, the only adult influence in the class is usually the teacher. What could happen if teens and adults were in the same classroom learning *with* each other and from each other's experiences and insights? Teens would be able to hear the thoughts of adults as they wrestle with tough topics. This level of sharing and vulnerability can benefit your teens' spiritual maturation process immensely. When a church offers Christian education that combines youth and adults, it helps to build bridges between generations.

A ministry to families with teens can also involve some educational opportunities for parents. The church can offer classes on sex education, communication, discipline, drugs and alcohol, discerning right from wrong, youth culture, discipleship, and building their teen's self-esteem. You can teach these sessions, or you can bring in other church staff or outside sources. Many of these educational experiences can be applicable to a setting that combines parents with their teens.

Evangelism and Discipleship / Earlier we looked at how evangelism and discipleship are part of a ministry to families with teens. These two categories play out in every area of your programming. No matter what the event, either evangelism or discipleship is occurring—and often times both! Take every opportunity to allow the Holy Spirit to do His work in the lives of the parents and teens in your ministry.

Recreation / As you program for recreation, pull your game books off the shelf. Any game that works with your teens will work with parents and teens. When you put parents and teens together for recreation, you are showing teens that Christian adults love to laugh and have fun. Parents and teens can play volleyball, softball, and football; go skiing, bowling, biking, and hiking; enjoy hayrides, rappelling, picnics, concerts, and board games—*together.* Anything you can do with teens you can do with parents and teens!

In my mind a truly cooperative church does more than provide seminars on family-related topics, however basic they may be. A cooperative church defines its role in such a way that it genuinely serves its members by actively strengthening their families.

Dennis Guernsey
A New Design for Family Ministry

Total Programming

So, how does this look when all the elements are put

together? Part 3 includes a sample of a four-year cycle of programming for parents and teens. This chart is divided by preteen, junior high, and senior high developmental stages to help provide continuity in your ministry. Don't feel that you have to put all of these programs into place in the first year; this is just a sample. Make yours fit the uniqueness of your ministry setting. Phase your program in slowly as your group of parents and teens are ready for each part.

*O*ur goal should be to enable families to become strong and healthy so they'll have the inner resources to cope with stresses they'll inevitably face.
Dub Ambrose and Walt Mueller
Ministry to Families with Teenagers, 82

You see it really *does* take a family to raise a youth ministry! Raise the standard of your youth ministry. Advance His kingdom. The race is yours for the running. "Run in such a way as to get the prize" (1 Corinthians 9:24).

On your mark . . . get set . . . go!

Part three

Practical Tools for Your Ministry

Ministry to Families with Teens
Four-Year Planning Cycle

	Year One	**Year Two**
Preteen (6th Grade)	• *Family Sunday School:* "Preparing for Adolescence" • *Family Service Project:* Clothes Pantry • *Parent Seminar:* "Building Self-esteem in Your Teen" • *Family Recreation:* Amusement Park Trip	• *Family Sunday School:* "Basic Training" • *Family Service Project:* Clean a Community Park • *Parent Seminar:* "New Roles, New Rules" • *Family Recreation:* Trip to the Zoo
Junior High (7th and 8th Grade)	• *Family Sunday School:* Study of Romans • *Family Service Project:* Serve at Soup Kitchen • *Parent Seminar:* "Help! My Kid's a Teen!" (youth culture) • *Family Recreation:* Family Olympics • *Family Mission Trip:* Inner-city Work and Witness	• *Family Sunday School:* Study of Galatians and Ephesians • *Family Service Project:* Nursing Home • *Parent Seminar:* "Building Better Communication" • *Family Recreation:* Family Game Night • *Family Mission Trip:* Inner-city Work and Witness
Senior High (9th-12th Grades)	• *Family Sunday School:* Study of Acts • *Family Service Project:* Habitat for Humanity House • *Parent Seminar:* "Help! My Kid's a Teen!" (youth culture) • *Family Recreation:* Parent/Teen Match Game • *Mission Trip:* Out-of-Stater (encourage parental participation)	• *Family Sunday School:* Study of 1 Corinthians • *Family Service Project:* Community Cleanup • *Parent Seminar:* "Building Self-esteem in Your Teen" • *Family Recreation:* Family Ropes Course • *Mission Trip:* Out-of-Stater (encourage parental participation)

	Year Three	**Year Four**
Preteen	• *Repeat Year One* (parental participation)	• *Repeat Year Two* (parental participation)
Junior High	• *Family Sunday School:* Study of John • *Family Service Project:* Clean a Community Park • *Parent Seminar:* "New Roles, New Rules" • *Family Recreation:* Role Reversal Night • *Family Mission Trip:* Inner-city Work and Witness	• *Family Sunday School:* Study of Philippians and Colossians • *Family Service Project:* Serve at a Soup Kitchen • *Parent Seminar:* "Building Self-esteem in Your Teen" • *Family Recreation:* Family Game Night • *Family Mission Trip:* Inner-city Work and Witness
Senior High	• *Family Sunday School:* Study of 1 and 2 Timothy and James • *Family Service Project:* Elderly House Repair/Cleaning • *Parent Seminar:* "Helping Your Teen Grow Spiritually" • *Family Activity:* "Family Olympics" • *Mission Trip:* Out-of-Stater (encourage parental participation)	• *Family Sunday School:* Study of 1 and 2 Thessalonians • *Family Service Project:* Children's Hospital Clown Ministry • *Parent Seminar:* "Preparing for the Future" • *Family Activity:* Hiking/Camping Trip • *Mission Trip:* Out-of-Stater (encourage parental participation)

Ready-to-Use Parent/Teen Talks

*T*his section contains practical tools to help you conduct parent and teen talks on a variety of topics in settings such as meetings, retreats, or classes. Written by veteran youth workers who are committed to family ministry, these ready-to-use talks will be beneficial to you in the development of your ministry to families with teens.

Building Rules Without Burning Bridges

Wayne Rice
Director, Understanding Your Teenager
and Cofounder of Youth Specialties

- *"Be home on weekend nights by 11:00."*
- *"No friends in the house when we're not home . . . except for Janie Fredrickson."*
- *"Put all your dirty laundry in the laundry basket by Monday morning or it won't get washed."*
- *"No phone calls after 10 P.M."*
- *"No watching MTV."*

Parents, what rules do you have for your teenage children? Chances are you have plenty. As your kids become teens, there is definitely a need for more rules—not so much because teens are rebellious, but because teens want to know your expectations.

When they were little, you were able to act as a benevolent dictator, simply ordering your children around. But now that they're older, that approach won't work. They want to know what the rules are (in advance), and they want to know why they're expected to obey them.

Will teens obey the rules that you put in place for them? Believe it or not, the vast majority of teens actually *want* rules. Few teens like living in homes without limits or guidance. But to make those rules work in your home, here are five simple, but effective, guidelines:

1. **Make sure the rules are reasonable.** If you want your teen to pay attention to your rules and obey them, make them reasonable. If one rule is stupid, your teen may start thinking that all the rules are stupid. A popular saying nowadays is "Don't sweat the small stuff," and it applies here. Don't ask your teen to obey rules that are trivial or impossible. The best approach is to discuss any proposed rule and listen to your teen's objections. This doesn't mean your teen must like the rule, but he or she will at least know that you have considered his or her point of view. This increases the probability of compliance.

2. **Make sure the rules are clear.** If you can't be specific about rules, don't make them. Vague rules are bound to be broken. If you tell a teen to come home early from an activity, you are setting the teen up for failure. Early? What's early? Or: "Clean your room!" What exactly does "clean" mean? Your teen may think that shoving dirty clothes under the bed, revealing at least four square feet of floor, is "clean." You'd have to admit, it's cleaner than it was!

3. **Make sure the rules have consequences that your teen understands in advance.** What happens if a rule is broken? You don't want to be put into the position of having to respond to disobedience with yelling, anger, or punishment that is usually emotional and arbitrary. Your teen should understand that any decision to disobey a rule is a decision to accept a clear consequence that is reasonable and that has been agreed upon in advance. This will relieve you from having to react (or overreact) when a rule is broken. If a curfew rule is broken, for example, you can simply say, "I see you have decided to stay home for the next two weeks. I accept your decision, and I'll make sure your wishes are granted."

4. **Keep a warm relationship with your teen.** Rules won't act as glue to keep your family close, but relationships will. Take time to do things with your teen that he or she enjoys. Treat your teen with the same kind of dignity and respect with which you would treat your adult friends. Find ways to keep the communication lines open. Do lunch. Take a trip together. Listen more. Just as teens do better in school for teachers they like, so they will be more likely to obey the rules at home if they have a good relationship with the rule maker.

5. Catch your teen in the act of doing something good.

Don't just criticize your teen when he or she messes up, but let it be known when he or she is doing well. If you affirm positive behavior, chances are pretty good that it will be repeated. Praise your teen often, even though he or she will more than likely respond with a shrug. Down deep your teen really does want your approval.

Parents, as long as your children are in your care, you have the God-given responsibility to give them the guidance and direction that they need (1 Timothy 3:4). Don't shy away from setting rules for your teenage children simply because you think they are too big to spank. But as you change the kind of rules you have, remember also to change the nature of the relationship that you have with your kids. Don't "exasperate" them (Ephesians 6:4) by treating them like children or being unreasonable. Give your kids lots of love, understanding, and support. And then expect obedience. You'll probably get it.

───────────────────────

For more info on Understanding Your Teenager or to contact Wayne regarding speaking to your parents and teens, contact him at:

Understanding Your Teenager
P.O. Box 420
Lakeside, CA 92040
800-561-9309
Web site: http://www.uyt.com

LOVE IN A HEALTHY FAMILY

Chap Clark

Associate Professor of Youth and Family Ministry
Fuller Theological Seminary

- **Play James Taylor's song "Shower the People" to open the talk.**

To have a radical family, you need to learn how to radically love! Has the following ever happened in your family? "I love you," your mom says as you move toward the door. "Love you too," you casually respond as the door shuts behind you.

Not every family says it, you know. Some just save the "I love yous" for special occasions—birthday cards, anniversaries, and holidays. But then there are families like mine (or my wife's) where you can't move from one room to another without somebody saying, "I love you!"

Whether you say it a lot or not, the idea behind these most-famous three little words can almost become empty of meaning in our fast-paced, cliché-filled culture. So, what does it mean to *really* love the members of your family?

When we examine the life of Jesus, we see love in action; and not only His love but sometimes that of those around Him showing us what real love looks like.

- **Read John 12:1-3.**

Mary loved Jesus, and she wanted to show Him how much she loved Him with a simple act. Let's look at four characteristics of genuine love that Mary displayed that day to let the world—and especially Jesus—know how real her love was:

First, **love is active.** Notice that Mary decided to do more than simply tell Jesus she loved Him—she *showed* Him! She didn't assume He knew. It is as if she had spent several minutes with all of this love energy, wanting to somehow go all out to make absolutely certain that Jesus was "showered" (as James Taylor sings) with love.

Second, **love is spontaneous.** In looking at this account, it is obvious that Mary didn't think too long and hard about this decision. There was no one in the next room egging her on. Pouring this expensive perfume on Jesus was not some kind of religious "duty dance" or obligation. (Sure, some commentators speculate that Mary was preparing Jesus for His burial, but there is absolutely no indication of that in the text!) She wanted to get His (and everyone else's) attention, and so she used the most precious and costly item at hand to show her love.

Third, **love is authentic.** It is never condescending or an act of arrogance and power. She didn't seem to really want to draw attention to *herself;* she just wanted to show her great and deep love for Jesus. You don't see here a "Hey, look at me, aren't I something" attitude or even a self-defending justification, "It really has been a great year for nard!" coming from Mary. Nope, she simply wanted to love Jesus. That's it.

And fourth, **love is extravagant.** That's the true beauty of this account. This was potent stuff! This was no ordinary, no-big-deal type of perfume. This was the eyes-watering, out-of-control, overkill, "Oh, she broke the flask!" type of love! Mary was going for broke to express her love for Jesus Christ.

Love is never wholly logical—but the Christian life only works when we are so captivated with the person of Christ and His gospel that it will show—in our families, our dating, our friendships, and our growth!

Do you love the individuals in your family? Don't just tell them so; *show them!* Make sure you *demonstrate* your love by being active, spontaneous, authentic, and extravagant!

Chap Clark is an author of numerous books and articles and speaks to youth, parents, and families. If you're looking for someone to speak to your youth, parents, or both, Chap can be reached at:

Fuller Theological Seminary
135 N. Oakland Ave.
Pasadena, CA 91182
626-584-5608
cclark@fuller.edu

The Gift of Discernment

Bob DeMoss
Entertainment Today, Inc.

Not long ago, I took part in a statewide church youth convention in Maine. I asked the 1,000 attendees to explain how they knew whether something was right or wrong. No kidding, it was five minutes of head scratching before someone spoke up. We were in trouble when the first youngster suggested, "I ask my dad."

"OK," I responded, "what if your dad were Adolf Hitler? Or, by contrast, what if your dad were Billy Graham? You'd most likely get two very different opinions of what was right and wrong behavior."

You could feel the audience wrestling with this issue of standards. (Keep in mind, this was a church youth convention.) I thought someone must have forgotten to coach them in the basics of their faith.

Finally, one youngster spoke up and inquired, "Oh, how about the Bible?" In the discussion that followed, I wanted them to understand how important their standard, the Bible, was and that any old standard wouldn't do. To make this point, I read from a copy of the "personal" section of a newspaper.

The first item said, "Attention couples! Interested in a threesome?" Another ad offered adultery: "Two businessmen seek married ladies to share occasional afternoons. Discretion assured." A total of five columns soliciting this sordid behavior was followed by a disclaimer: "We reserve the right to refuse or edit any personal ad that does not meet the standards of this publication."

Did this paper have standards? Actually, yes. They refused to accept ads for sex with children; that's the only form of behavior they considered out-of-bounds. Lesson one: not all standards are created equal.

Thus, the first step toward becoming a discerning thinker is to establish a reliable standard by which all of life is evaluated. I am fortunate that my parents elected to use the Bible as our family standard. But I'm stunned to learn how many Christian parents fail to teach their teens how to apply the principles of Scripture to real-life situations.

That's where you parents can provide an invaluable service. Here, then, are the seven attributes of a critical thinker to review with your teen. As you discuss these principles with your teen, incorporate current events (quotations; articles; even scenes from a popular TV show, CD, or film) to drive the point home:

A critical thinker:

1. Has a firmly developed sense of right and wrong and prefers wisdom to foolish thinking (Psalm 119:97-98, 101, 104-105).

2. Understands that not all forms of music, media, and entertainment are harmless fun (1 Peter 5:8).

3. Doesn't laugh or enjoy it, when his or her values are attacked, mocked, or undermined by popular culture (Colossians 3:1-2, 5-6; Romans 1:32).

4. Has a habit of asking probing questions about the choices he or she is considering (Jeremiah 17:9-10).

5. Desires to honor and please the Lord with the choices he or she makes (1 Peter 1:17-19).

6. Knows that God places a premium on proper communication (Matthew 12:36-37).

7. Is willing to suffer the loss of a specific entertainment option rather than allow hostile ideas to dominate his or her mind (Psalm 101:2-4).

You might also teach them this simple prayer: *Lord, help me to love what You love and hate what You hate.* As the Father grants this petition, we will enjoy a discerning spirit no matter the circumstance.

Bob DeMoss, author of Learn to Discern *and* 21 Days to Better Family Entertainment, *is an international speaker on youth culture. If you would like more information on his video or seminar on popular entertainment, contact Bob at:*

Entertainment Today, Inc.
P.O. Box 121, 228
Nashville, TN 37212

Why Teens Should Obey Their Parents

Tom Lytle
Minister to Families
Marion (Ohio) First Church of the Nazarene

It's difficult being a parent. It's difficult being a teen. It's *extremely* difficult being a parent of a teen. There are lots of books, experts, and advice givers out there, but sometimes parents just need to hang in there as they navigate the treacherous waters of adolescent growth and development.

God's Word can be a great source of advice and encouragement for teens and parents. Ephesians 6 offers some sound advice for both teens and their parents. Let's take a look at the teens' side of the equation and explore three reasons why teens should honor and obey their parents.

First, because it is right. Ephesians 6:1 says, "Children, obey your parents in the Lord, for this is right." And when the Scripture says it is right, it means it is right in an *absolute, moral sense* for all of us. When disobedience to parents becomes the norm of a culture, that culture is on a decline. It's interesting that in Romans 1:28-32 Paul has given us the consequence for much of today's culture: "Furthermore, since they did not think it worthwhile to retain the knowledge of God, he gave them over to a depraved mind, to do what ought not to be done. They have become filled with every kind of wickedness, evil, greed and depravity. They are full of envy, murder, strife, deceit and malice. They are gossips, slanderers, God-haters, insolent, arrogant and boastful; they invent ways of doing evil; they disobey their parents."

"They disobey their parents." Almost doesn't seem to fit, does it? "They are senseless, faithless, heartless, ruthless.

Although they know God's righteous decree . . . they not only continue to do these very things but also approve of those who practice them."

The Bible says it's also right in a *logical sense*. It only makes sense that teens should honor and obey their parents, given that parents brought teens into the world and have greater wisdom, knowledge, and experience than teens. It is to teens' benefit to obey their parents who are looking out for their children's best interests.

Second, because it is written. Ephesians 6:2 says, "'Honor your father and mother'—which is the first commandment with a promise." In the Ten Commandments, honoring your parents is listed fifth. The Ten Commandments can be divided into two sections: the first four commandments as our duty to God, and the last six commandments—beginning with honoring your parents—as our duty to others.

The Jews believe that Moses came down from the mountain with five commandments in each hand. For Jews, honoring and obeying one's parents falls under our duty to God. I think the Jews have it right. Moms and Dads, you have the awesome responsibility and obligation to represent God to your teens—to represent God's justice, to represent God's love, and to represent God's character to your teens—because their concepts of God are formed by you.

Third, because it is righteous. Paul inserts a very interesting clause into Ephesians 6:1. He says, "Children, obey your parents in the Lord." What is meant by "in the Lord"?

Some say Paul was placing a condition of obedience. However, Paul's flow of thought indicates that he has a Christian home in mind, not a situation where parental orders may be in conflict with the gospel.

Paul is indicating that teens should honor and obey their parents as an expression of their relationship with Jesus Christ. It is a new standard marked, not by grudging submission, but by loving respect. It's acknowledging that Christ has given parents authority over their teens. Parents, you accept and embrace them. You listen to them. You acknowledge their feelings. You love and you care for them. And teens, you seek to make your parents proud of you by your choices and your actions—in the Lord! And "in the Lord" means that you respect them with your tone of voice, your facial expressions, and the way you speak about them to others. Why? Because it's righteous. It's an expression of your personal relationship to Christ.

One of the common complaints of teens today is "My parents don't trust me." I ask, have you been honoring them in the Lord? I've come just short of saying that not honoring and not obeying your parents is not only wrong but a sin. Whenever sin is involved, confession and repentance are the cure. So is this a sin that you need to confess and repent of?

Prayer: *Pray that God will continue to work in the relationships between parents and teens; that the relationship will be "in the Lord" and that teens would be able to love, respect, and obey their parents; and that the honor in this relationship would be like the honor we give to God through our lives.*

How to Really Love Your Teens

Tom Lytle
Minister to Families
Marion (Ohio) First Church of the Nazarene

College and Careers magazine surveyed teens recently, asking them who they admire the most. Only 7 percent of teen girls said they admire Hillary Clinton. Eleven percent said they admire Oprah Winfrey. But 79 percent said they admire their mothers.

Only 8 percent of teen boys admire President Clinton. Twelve percent admire various movie stars. But 73 percent said they admire their dads.

Parents, think about that. *You are your teen's heroes!*

To be a good hero you need to know how to love your teens. Ephesians 6:4 offers words of encouragement and advice to parents who want to be their teen's hero. "Fathers, do not exasperate your children; instead, bring them up in the training and instruction of the Lord." By the way, the word translated for fathers is an inclusive word. Paul clearly has in mind both fathers and mothers.

First, Paul looks at the negative. Parents, if you really love your teens, you must first eliminate exasperation. "To exasperate" means "to frustrate and discourage." It's that feeling of *I can't do anything right!*

So just what about parenting exasperates teens? Here's a list of five ways parents can exasperate their teens.

- Demanding a standard of behavior for your teen but not exhibiting that standard in your own lives

- Always blaming and never praising your teen

- Breaking your promises

- Making no allowance for the immaturity and inexperience of your teen

- Having a controlling, manipulative style of parenting that suppresses rather than encourages development

Paul quickly follows up this negative directive with a positive one. He says, "Instead, bring them up in the training and instruction of the Lord." The same word for "bring them up" is translated as "nourish" or "feed." Parents need to feed their teens spiritually. *And teens can eat a lot.*

Then Paul calls parents to training; he suggests that teens need two types of training in their lives. One to let them know when they've done well, to encourage them. And one to let them know when they've done wrong, to discourage inappropriate behavior. Teens need boundaries and limits to feel secure.

The second call to parents is instruction. *Instruction* literally means "to impart understanding with a focus on the will and the attitude." Parents are to inspire their teen's behaviors and attitudes. I asked myself: *How can we do that?* Here's a list of 10 ways you can inspire your teen's behaviors and attitudes.

- I will always love and respect my teen for who he is and not for who I want him to be.

- I will give my teen space to grow, to dream, to succeed, and even (sometimes) to fail.

- I will create a loving home environment and show my teen that she is loved wherever and however I can.

- I will discipline when necessary and let my teen know that I disapprove of *what he does* but not *who he is.*

- I will set limits for my teen and help her discover security in knowing what is expected of her.

- I will make time for my teen and cherish our moments together.

- I will not burden my teen with emotions and problems he is not equipped to deal with, by remembering that I am the parent and he is the teen.

- I will encourage my teen to experience the world and all its possibilities by guiding her in its ways and taking pains to teach her to be careful but not fearful.

- I will take care of myself physically and emotionally so that I can be there for my teen when he needs me.

- I will try to be the kind of person I want my teen to grow up to be—loving, fair-minded, moral, giving, and hopeful.

So parents, do you really want to love your teens? Eliminate exasperation by training and instructing your teens in the teachings of the Lord. You will set into motion a victorious cycle of gentle nurturing, obedience, trust, and freedom by following this pattern. That victorious cycle will replace the vicious cycle of rebellion, punishment, anger, and suspicion that each of us fears as parents.

Family Survey

Identify those families in your church and/or community that include teenagers. Mail a copy of the following survey to each member of the family (12 years or older), and allow approximately one week to complete the survey. After the surveys have been returned to you, go through them and calculate the responses to see what the "hot buttons" are for your families with teens; you may wish to have the members of your Family Committee assist you in this process. You may also want to repeat the survey once every year in order to stay current with the needs of the families in your church and community.

You will find it helpful to attach a cover letter to each survey, explaining in more detail who you are, exactly why you're conducting the survey, and what information you hope to obtain through the responses. You may wish to pattern this letter after the following example:

The youth ministry department of [your church name] desires to help meet the needs of families with teens in our church and our surrounding community. In order to help us know how to better serve you, please have each member of your family complete the following survey. You won't be required to write your name or any other identifying personal information on this survey, so please respond freely, knowing that your answers will be kept in strict confidence. The information from this survey will be compiled into one report that will be made available to you in the future at your request.

Thank you for participating in this survey. It will help us better minister to the needs of you and your family.

Sincerely,

[Your Name]

Family Survey

Please check (✔) the appropriate box:

1. Are you: □ A teen's mom   □ A teen's stepmom
             □ A teen's dad   □ A teen's stepdad
             □ A teen   □ Other: _____

2. How old are you: □ 12-14   □ 31-40
                     □ 15-17   □ 41-50
                     □ 18-25   □ 51-60
                     □ 26-30   □ Over 60

━━━━━ **Family Life** ━━━━━

3. On a scale of 1 to 10 (10 being "totally satisfied") how would you rate your satisfaction with your family?

   Circle one: 1   2   3   4   5   6   7   8   9   10

4. On a scale of 1 to 10 (10 being "total satisfaction") how much satisfaction would you like to have in your family?

   Circle one: 1   2   3   4   5   6   7   8   9   10

5. Which of the following would improve your answer to question No. 3?

   □ Spending more time together   □ Talking openly more often
   □ Sharing more responsibilities □ Having more money
   □ Getting along better with each other   □ Other: _____

6. In which of the following areas do you feel your family needs improvement? *(Mark all that apply.)*

   □ Open communication   □ Trust
   □ Respecting privacy   □ Sharing our faith
   □ Discipline   □ Setting expectations
   □ Defining rules   □ Showing affection
   □ Having fun together   □ Defined roles
   □ Family worship   □ Serving others
   □ Negotiating roles and rules   □ Other: _____

7. Which of the following family problems does your family deal with, and how often?

	All the time	Often	Occasionally	Never
Lack of communication	☐	☐	☐	☐
Alcohol abuse	☐	☐	☐	☐
Drug abuse	☐	☐	☐	☐
Parent-teen arguments	☐	☐	☐	☐
Marital problems	☐	☐	☐	☐
Sibling arguments	☐	☐	☐	☐
Stress at home	☐	☐	☐	☐
Personal stress	☐	☐	☐	☐
Religious differences	☐	☐	☐	☐
School problems	☐	☐	☐	☐
Juvenile delinquency	☐	☐	☐	☐
Physical/sexual abuse	☐	☐	☐	☐
Other: _____	☐	☐	☐	☐

8. What is your religious affiliation?

☐ A member of this church (if so, for how long? ___)

☐ A regular attendee of this church (if so, for how long? ___)

☐ Member or regular attendee of another church

☐ Not a regular attendee of any church

☐ Not religious

9. On a scale of 1 to 10 (10 being "very important") rate the importance of your faith and church involvement to your family?

Circle one: 1   2   3   4   5   6   7   8   9   10

10. How often do you attend church activities?

☐ Once a week   ☐ Occasionally   ☐ Once a month

☐ Rarely   ☐ Never

11. On a scale of 1 to 10 (10 being "couldn't be better") how would you rate the ability of this church's current programming to meet the needs of your family?

Circle one: 1   2   3   4   5   6   7   8   9   10

12. If this church provided programs offering assistance in any of the following areas, which would you or your family consider participating in? *(Mark all that apply.)*

- ☐ Parent-teen relationships
- ☐ Making a family budget
- ☐ Time management
- ☐ Solving family conflict
- ☐ Blended families
- ☐ Single parenting
- ☐ Dealing with divorce
- ☐ Setting expectations
- ☐ Family worship
- ☐ Family communication
- ☐ Stepfamily relations
- ☐ Teaching values
- ☐ Coping with stress
- ☐ Marriage enrichment
- ☐ Teaching teens about sex
- ☐ Negotiating rules and roles
- ☐ Drug and alcohol abuse
- ☐ Discipline in the family
- ☐ Other: _____

13. Which of the following family activities would you consider attending if sponsored by this church?

- ☐ Family picnic
- ☐ Family talent show
- ☐ Family retreat (one day)
- ☐ Family worship service
- ☐ Family service projects
- ☐ Family Bible study
- ☐ Family game night
- ☐ Family retreat (overnight)
- ☐ Family Olympics
- ☐ Family Sunday School
- ☐ Family mission trips
- ☐ Other:
- ☐ I would not attend church-sponsored programs/activities.

14. When is the best time for you to attend family activities and/or workshops?

- ☐ Weekdays during the day
  (list days most preferable: _____)
- ☐ Weekday evenings
  (list days most preferable: _____)
- ☐ Saturday mornings
- ☐ Saturday afternoons
- ☐ Saturday evenings
- ☐ Sunday mornings
- ☐ Sunday afternoons
- ☐ Sunday evenings

15. How often would you be interested in attending family activities and workshops?

- ☐ Once a week
- ☐ Once a month
- ☐ Once a year
- ☐ Every other week
- ☐ Once every quarter
- ☐ Never

16. What are some important ways this church could help your family?

_____

_____

_____

_____

_____

_____

For Teens Only

(Parents go to question 25.)

17. What grade are you in?

☐ 6th   ☐ 7th   ☐ 8th   ☐ 9th

☐ 10th   ☐ 11th   ☐ 12th

☐ High school graduate attending college

☐ High school graduate not attending college

18. Do you work outside your home? _____
    If so, how many hours per week? _____

19. List any after-school activities you're involved in:

_____

_____

_____

_____

20. What is the marital status of your parents?

Father: ☐ Single   ☐ Married   ☐ Divorced

           ☐ Remarried   ☐ Widowed   ☐ Deceased

Mother: ☐ Single   ☐ Married   ☐ Divorced

           ☐ Remarried   ☐ Widowed   ☐ Deceased

21. With whom do you live?

☐ Both parents   ☐ My grandparent(s)

☐ My mom   ☐ My mom and stepdad

☐ My dad   ☐ My dad and stepmom

☐ Other: _____

How many brothers and/or sisters also live with you?

☐ Brothers _____   ☐ Sisters _____

22. What is the one issue that causes the most conflict between you and your parent(s)?

_____

_____

_____

_____

23. What do you like the most about your parent(s)?

_____

_____

_____

_____

_____

24. If you could tell your parents one thing, what would it be?

_____

_____

_____

_____

_____

For Parents Only

(Teens go to question 34.)

25. What is your marital status?

☐ Never Married   ☐ Married *(first marriage)*

☐ Remarried   ☐ Separated

☐ Divorced   ☐ Widowed

☐ Other:

26. How long have you been married to your present spouse?
_____ years

27. Which best describes your occupation?

☐ Homemaker   ☐ Self-employed   ☐ Unemployed

☐ Skilled trade *(carpenter, electrician, technician, etc.)*

☐ Professional *(teacher, doctor, lawyer, etc.)*

☐ Retired

28. Which best describes your spouse's occupation?

☐ Homemaker   ☐ Self-employed   ☐ Unemployed

☐ Skilled trade *(carpenter, electrician, technician, etc.)*

☐ Professional *(teacher, doctor, lawyer, etc.)*

☐ Retired

☐ Unmarried

29. How many hours do you work in an average week? _____

30. How many children do you have? _____
    What are their ages? _____

31. What is the one issue that causes the most conflict between you and your teen(s)?

_____

_____

_____

_____

32. What do you like the most about your teen(s)?

_____

_____

_____

33. If you could tell your teen one thing, what would it be?

_____

_____

_____

_____

Comments

34. Do you have any additional comments or questions for us? If so, list them here or you can call us at _____.

_____

_____

_____

   Thank you for taking the time to complete this survey. We are here to serve you, and this survey will help us to better focus our ministry to fit your needs.

Selecting a Christian Counselor

Counseling, especially family counseling, has become more commonplace for a large sector of our society. There are many different types of counselors specializing in many different areas. There are both Christian and non-Christian experts in just about every field of counseling. So when a family comes to you looking for a "good" counselor, how do you help that family locate the "right" counselor for them and their situation? Does your church have a relationship with a good Christian counselor to whom you can make referrals? If not, perhaps the following will assist you in building a positive relationship with a counselor to whom you can entrust your families.

What are the different types of counselors? What should you look for in a counselor? How will you know you have found one you can trust? Well, let's look into this.

Recently I pulled out my local phone book and looked under "Counselors" and discovered a long list of "See . . ." The list included Alcoholism Treatment, Child and Adolescent Guidance Counselors, Financial Planning, Marriage and Family Counselors, Psychologists, Psychotherapists, Religious Counseling, Social Workers, and many others. I tried to think as if I was looking for a counselor to whom I would refer a family of one of the teens from my youth group. So I looked under "Religious Counseling" for more help, and I found 10 listings for either Christian counseling centers or Christian counselors. Now that I've narrowed the list of numerous counselors to just 10, the work begins. If I am going to refer one of my families to one of these, I need to know something about the counselors.

Now it's time to let my fingers do the walking—time to reach out and touch someone, if you know what I mean. But wait! What am I going to ask them? What am I going to say, that "a *friend of mine* needs to see a counselor"? Yeah, as if they're going to buy that line! Seriously, what do I ask them?

How will I know I can trust them with one of my families? Maybe the following list of questions will help:

1. *What is their education? Where did they go to school? What degrees do they hold? What theory of counseling were they taught, and which do they follow?*

This is extremely important. If a counselor doesn't have the appropriate credentials to do counseling, thank the person for his or her time and move on to the next counselor on your list. Believe it or not, some states will allow just about anyone to hang a shingle out front and call himself or herself a therapist. But if a person isn't properly trained, the person isn't worth your time.

So, what training is sufficient? A master's degree in a counseling field is a minimum. Social workers and marriage and family therapists are not required to possess a doctorate to practice. The same applies to master's-level psychologists, but the American Psychological Association still requires them to work under the supervision of a Ph.D. psychologist.

When it comes to theories of counseling, it will be important for you to locate a counselor who is trained in family systems theory. This approach looks at the whole family and how the members relate to one another. When examining families, family systems theory believes that the whole is greater than the sum of its parts—which simply means that the family is greater as a unit than as a group of disconnected individuals.

2. *What licensure(s) do they have? To which counseling organizations and associations do they belong?*

Many states have licensures for the many different types of counselors. Sometimes licensure laws have either not been drawn up or not been passed by the state legislature for some of the types of counseling. The minimum a consumer should expect from a counselor is that the counselor be registered with the state and belong to a legitimate crediting association. Some examples of associations for counselors include the American Psychological Association, the National Association of Social Workers, the American Association of Marriage and Family Therapy, the American Association of Pastoral Counselors, and the American Association of Christian Counselors. Many of these associations have state chapters that counselors should belong to as well. Any credible association has a written code of ethics that its members must adhere to. It would be helpful to have a copy of the association's code of ethics. If the counselor is unable to give you a copy, request a phone number where you can call to request a copy. This will help you more closely examine the standards of this counselor.

3. Do they work under the supervision of another counselor? If so, what are that person's qualifications?

Supervision should not be looked upon as a weakness; rather, it is a system of counselors making themselves accountable to each other for the counseling they do. Remember, "As iron sharpens iron, so one [counselor] sharpens another." Make sure the supervisor is a qualified supervisor, though, and has gone through sufficient training to be a supervisor.

4. What is their specialization? Do they do individual, group, and/or family counseling? Do they work with families with teens?

Every counselor has an area of expertise. You need to make sure that a counselor's area is the area you are looking for. This also means that you might need to do your homework ahead of time so that you have a list of experts ready for different areas of counseling. Some examples of areas of expertise are eating disorders, drug abuse and alcoholism, domestic violence, adolescents, families (some counselors specialize in different types of issues within the family realm), mental illness, sexual dysfunction, juvenile delinquency, behavior problems, ADD/ADHD, marital issues, and the list goes on. In fact, it seems as if there are counselors for just about every kind of counseling one might need.

5. For how long do they generally see clients? And how often? How long will the treatment take?

Counseling can be a long process or it can be brief, depending on the counselor and the specific case. Insurance companies have been pushing counselors to do brief counseling with their clients. Brief counseling can be a six- to eight-session plan of treatment, with defined and attainable goals. The old method of being in counseling for what seemed a lifetime is going by the wayside, and people are looking for results that can be reached in a short-term time frame.

This brings up another important issue. You need to ask the counselors if they use and follow a treatment plan with defined goals in their counseling. Not only should they use these, but they need to allow their clients to take an active part in developing the treatment plan, setting goals, and evaluating when the goals have been reached.

6. *Do they use biblical principles in the counseling setting?*

Remember, just because counselors say they are Christian counselors doesn't mean they will use biblical principles in the counseling sessions. Also be aware that some "Christian" accrediting associations will grant someone a membership in their association without requiring that person to possess theological training [education] before they're allowed to practice theological counseling. Some people are "Christian counselors" simply because they are Christians. Make sure they have a firm grasp on theology before you consider them.

7. *What are their fees for service?*

Some counselors are able to accept insurance as payment or partial payment for their services. Others offer their services on a sliding scale, which means they adjust their rates according to the family's income. It might be good to note which counselors accept insurance and which insurance companies they accept. Most families would be appreciative of your efforts in knowing this information in advance.

8. *Can clients call them between sessions in case of emergencies?*

Some counselors do not like to be called between sessions with a family, as this can lead to the family becoming too dependent upon the counselor. But in the case of an emergency, most counselors will accept calls from a client. Also, make certain the counselor has a backup plan in case of emergencies when either the office is closed or the counselor is out of town.

Remember that many counselors are experts in their fields. You might want to invite them to come to your church to speak to your teens, parents, families, or church on a topic relating to their specialties. Many times counselors will come for little or no pay, assuming they'll either gain a few clients from the engagement or that you will become a source for future referrals. When you're looking for someone to come to your church to talk about family relations, communications, or whatever you need, you might want to consider a Christian counselor in your community who specializes in one of these areas.

For Further Reference

Ambrose, Dub, and Walt Mueller. *Ministry to Families with Teenagers.* Loveland, Colo.: Group Publishing, 1988.

Barna, George. *Generation Next.* Ventura, Calif.: Regal Books, 1995.

Borthwick, Paul. *Organizing Your Youth Ministry.* Grand Rapids: Zondervan Publishing House, 1988.

Clark, Chap. *The Youth Worker's Handbook to Family Ministry.* Grand Rapids: Zondervan Publishing House, 1997.

Covey, Stephen R. *The Seven Habits of Highly Effective Families.* New York: Golden Books, 1997.

DeMoss, Robert G., Jr. *Learn to Discern.* Grand Rapids: Zondervan, 1997.

———. *21 Days to Better Family Entertainment.* Grand Rapids: Zondervan, 1998.

DeVries, Mark. *Family-Based Youth Ministry.* Downer's Grove, Ill.: InterVarsity Press, 1994.

Doherty, William J., Ph.D. *The Intentional Family.* New York: Addison-Wesley Publishing, 1997.

Fields, Doug. *Purpose Driven Youth Ministry.* Grand Rapids: Zondervan, 1998.

Guernsey, Dennis. *A New Design for Family Ministry.* Elgin, Ill.: David C. Cook, 1992.

Larson, Jim. *A Church Guide for Strengthening Families.* Minneapolis: Augsburg, 1984.

Lytle, Tom, Kelly Schwartz, and Gary Hartke. *101 Ways to Be Family-Friendly in Youth Ministry.* Kansas City: Beacon Hill Press of Kansas City, 1996.

Rahn, Dave. "Parafamily Youth Ministry." *Group* magazine, May/June 1996, 36-39.

Sell, Charles. *Family Ministry.* Grand Rapids: Zondervan, 1995.

Stinnett, Nicholas. "Six Qualities That Make Families Strong." in *Family Building: Six Qualities of a Strong Family,* ed. George Rekers. Ventura, Calif.: Regal Books, 1985.

Westerhoff, John. *Bringing Up Children in the Faith.* Minneapolis: Winston, 1980.

Notes

1. Mark DeVries, *Family-Based Youth Ministry* (Downers Grove, Ill.: InterVarsity Press, 1994), 79.

2. U.S. Department of Commerce, Bureau of the Census, *Statistical Abstract of the United States—1996* (Washington, D.C.: GPO, 1996), 6.

3. Charles Sell, *Family Ministry* (Grand Rapids: Zondervan, 1995), 158.

4. Ibid., 15.

5. Nicholas Stinnett, "Six Qualities That Make Families Strong," in *Family Building: Six Qualities of a Strong Family,* ed. George Rekers (Ventura, Calif.: Regal Books, 1985), 38.

6. Sell, *Family Ministry,* 259-87.

7. George Barna, *Generation Next* (Ventura, Calif.: Regal Books, 1995), 69.

8. Ibid., 79.